Searchlight BOOKS™

How
Do Simple
Machines Work?

Put
Pulleys
to the Test

Sally M. Walker and Roseann Feldmann

Lerner Publications Company
Minneapolis

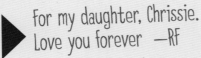

For my daughter, Chrissie.
Love you forever —RF

Lerner Publications Company
A division of Lerner Publishing Group, Inc.
241 First Avenue North
Minneapolis, MN 55401 U.S.A.

Website address: www.lernerbooks.com

Library of Congress Cataloging-in-Publication Data

Walker, Sally M.
    Put pulleys to the test / by Sally M. Walker and Roseann Feldmann.
        p.   cm. — (Searchlight books™—How do simple machines work?)
    Includes index.
    ISBN 978-0-7613-5322-5 (lib. bdg. : alk. paper)
    1. Pulleys—Juvenile literature. 2. Friction—Experiments—Juvenile literature.
  3. Gravity—Experiments—Juvenile literature. 4. Force and energy—Experiments—Juvenile literature. I. Feldmann, Roseann. II. Title.
    TJ1103.W352 2012
    621.8—dc22   2010035395

Manufactured in the United States of America
1 – DP – 7/15/11

Contents

Chapter 1

WORK

You work every day. When you raise window blinds, you are working. Playing and eating snacks are work too!

Eating fruit is work. What does the word *work* mean to a scientist?

You work when
you play cards!

Work = Using Force to Move an Object

When scientists use the word *work*, they don't mean the
opposite of play. Work is using a force to move an object.
Force is a push or a pull. You use force to play, to eat,
and to do chores.

This mother is pushing her son from one place to another. She is doing work.

Every time your force moves an object, you have done work. It does not matter how far the object moves. If it moves, work has been done.

If the object has not moved, you have not done work. It does not matter how hard you tried.

This boy is pushing on a house as hard as he can. But he can't move the house. So he is not doing work.

Chapter 2

MACHINES

Most people want their work to be easy. Machines are tools that make it easier to do work. Some machines make work go faster too.

Complicated Machines

Some machines have many moving parts. These machines are called complicated machines. Cranes and cars are complicated machines.

Cranes are machines that have many moving parts. What do we call machines that have many moving parts?

Simple Machines

Some machines have few moving parts. These machines are called simple machines. Simple machines are found in every home, school, and playground. They are so simple that most people do not realize they are machines.

This girl is using a simple machine to open window blinds.

Chapter 3
GRAVITY

Simple machines make your work easier. Some simple machines do this by changing the direction of your force. Pulling upward is hard work. Pulling downward is much easier. It is easier because gravity helps you. Gravity is the force that pulls everything toward Earth.

Lifting a heavy box is hard work. Why is it easier to lower the box to the ground?

Some simple machines change an upward force into a downward force. These machines make your work much easier.

When you drop a book, gravity pulls it to the floor. The book stays there until a stronger force moves it.

Gravity is pulling this book toward the floor.

Try This!

Put a heavy book on the floor. Lift it onto a table. Lifting the book is hard work. You must use a lot of force. Your lifting force has to be stronger than the pull of gravity.

Put the book back on the floor. It is much easier to lower the book than to lift it. When you lower the book, gravity helps you.

Gravity makes lifting a heavy book hard work.

If your force is in the same direction as gravity, your work is easier. You can prove this.

YOU WILL NEED A SCREWDRIVER, AN EMPTY POP-TOP CAN, SOME SMALL STONES OR SAND, A BIG PAPER CLIP, AND A PIECE OF STRING THAT IS 4 FEET (1 METER) LONG.

What You Do

Bend the ring on the can
until it sticks straight up.
Fill the can with stones or
sand. Hook the paper clip
on the ring. Tie a loop
at one end of the string.
The loop should be big
enough to fit loosely
around your hand.

Lift the ring on the
can, but don't break it
off. Then fill the can
with stones or sand.

Hook the loop of string onto the paper clip. Now put the can on the floor. Hold the string. Pull up on the string to lift the can onto the table. You must use a lot of force to lift the can. How much force must you use?

Hold the string, and lift the can onto the table.

This can is hanging from a spring scale. A spring scale measures force. The scale says the girl is using about 6 units of force to lift the can.

Next, put your screwdriver on the table. Place it so the handle is on the table. The narrow shaft should hang over the edge of the table. Have a friend hold the handle of the screwdriver so it cannot move. Put the can on the floor under the screwdriver.

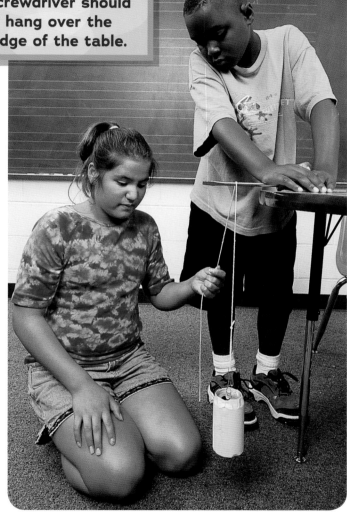

The shaft of your screwdriver should hang over the edge of the table.

Loop the string over the shaft of the screwdriver. When you pull down on the string, the can goes up. The can moves the same distance as it did when you pulled straight up.

But now your arm is pulling with gravity. Pulling with gravity makes your work easier.

The 6 units of force it takes to lift the can is the same as the force the other girl used to lift the can straight up. But this girl's work is easier because she is pulling down with gravity.

Chapter 4

FRICTION

When you pull the string, it rubs against the screwdriver. What kind of force does this make?

Raise and lower the can a few times. Notice how the string rubs against the shaft of the screwdriver. The rubbing between the string and the shaft makes friction. Friction is a force that slows or stops moving objects. Friction makes your can move more slowly. If there were less friction, your can would rise faster.

If you raise and lower the can many times, the string will start to wear out. Friction makes the string wear out.

Friction makes it hard to slide a heavy box on a sidewalk.

If there is less friction, the string will not wear out as quickly. How can you make less friction between the screwdriver and the string? Adding a wheel that spins is a great way to make less friction. You can make a spinning wheel with a spool and a rubber band.

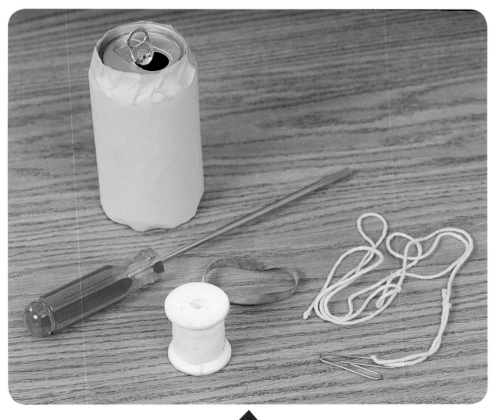

YOU CAN USE THESE OBJECTS TO EXPERIMENT WITH SPINNING WHEELS.

Now Try This!

Slide the spool around the shaft of your screwdriver. Wrap the rubber band around the tip of the screwdriver. This will keep the spool from sliding off. The spool is now a wheel. It is called a grooved wheel because the ridge at each side makes a groove around the middle. The wheel spins easily around the screwdriver. It spins easily because there is only a little friction between the spool and the screwdriver.

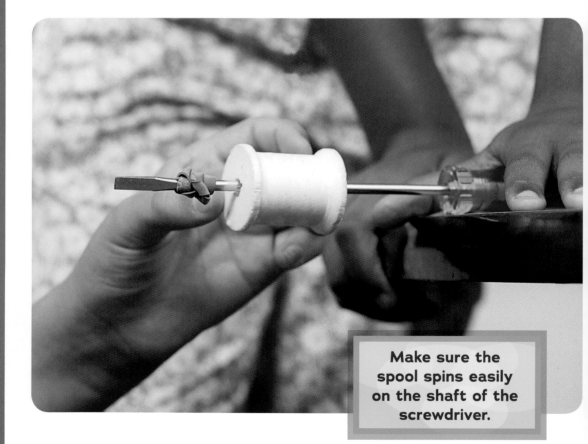

Make sure the spool spins easily on the shaft of the screwdriver.

Put the screwdriver back on the table. Have a friend hold it in place. The shaft and the wheel should hang over the edge of the table. Put the can on the floor under the screwdriver. This time, loop the string over the wheel.

Pull down on the string. The wheel and the string both move. There is very little friction. The can moves up really fast. Since the wheel and the string both move, the string rubs less. It will not wear out quickly.

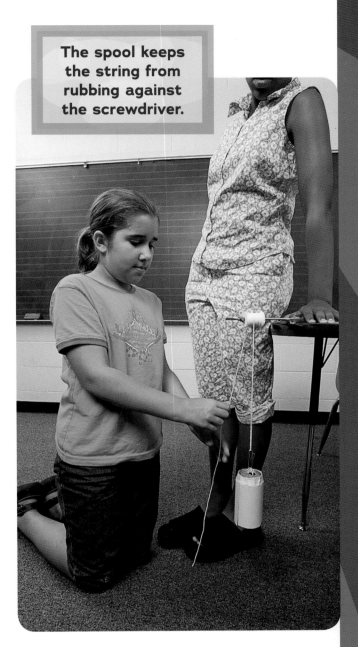

The spool keeps the string from rubbing against the screwdriver.

Chapter 5

KINDS OF PULLEYS

When you looped the string over the wheel, you made a pulley. A pulley is a simple machine. One end of your pulley's string is fastened to the can full of stones. The can is your pulley's load. A load is an object you want to move. The wheel of your pulley is grooved. The groove keeps the string from slipping off the wheel.

You have made a simple machine called a pulley! What kind of pulley did you make?

Fixed Pulleys

The pulley you made is called a fixed pulley. A fixed pulley stays attached in one place. It does not move.

A flagpole has a fixed pulley at the top. The flag is attached to a rope. The rope runs over the pulley. You pull down on one end of the rope. The flag goes up the pole. Using a fixed pulley to raise the flag makes your work easy.

A flagpole has a fixed pulley at the top.

Movable Pulleys

Another kind of pulley is called a movable pulley. A movable pulley does not stay in one place. A movable pulley is attached to a load. When the load moves, the pulley moves too. You use less force when you use a movable pulley than when you use a fixed pulley. Using less force makes your work easier.

This boy is holding onto a movable pulley. The pulley moves with him as he rides along the wire.

You can make a movable pulley with a sewing machine spool called a bobbin, two big paper clips, a straw, and the can and the string you used before.

A bobbin is a grooved wheel. Slide the bobbin onto the straw. Make sure the bobbin spins easily around the straw.

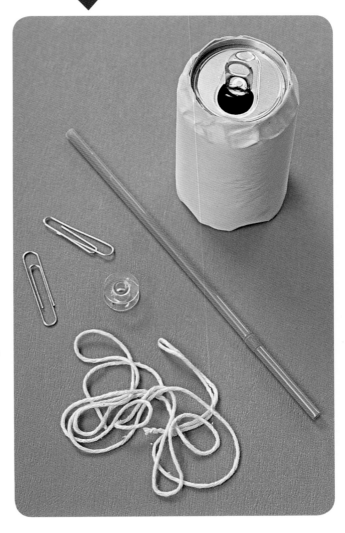

Hook both paper clips to the ring on your can. Slip one paper clip around one end of the straw. Slip the other paper clip around the other end of the straw. The bobbin will be between the two paper clips.

Wrap a piece of tape around each end of the straw. The tape will keep the bobbin and the paper clips from slipping off.

A loop is at the end of your string. Put the loop over a doorknob. Put the other end of the string around your bobbin. The bobbin becomes a movable pulley. Gently pull up on the string. Pull until the string begins to lift the pulley and the can.

Pull up on the string to lift the load.

The pulley and the load move together in a movable pulley.

Raise the end of the string up to the doorknob. See how the pulley rolls along the string. As the movable pulley moves, the load moves too. It's easy to lift the load with your movable pulley.

Think about your earlier lifts. First, you lifted the can straight up. Then you pulled down when you used your fixed pulley. The fixed pulley is the one that your friend held in place. Both times the load was hooked to one end of the string. You pulled on the other end. When you pulled, the load moved up. Both times you lifted the whole weight of the load yourself. You used a lot of force to do that.

Remember when you lifted the load with your fixed pulley? You used about 6 units of force to lift the load.

You use less force with your movable pulley. This girl is using about 3 units of force to lift the load.

You use less force to pull upward with your movable pulley than to pull downward with your fixed pulley. Why do you need to use less force with the movable pulley?

Look again at your movable pulley. The can is not hooked to the end of the string. The end of the string is attached to the doorknob. Lift the load again. You are not holding the whole load yourself. What else is helping you hold the load? The doorknob is helping you. You use less force because the doorknob holds some of the load's weight. Lifting less weight makes your work easier.

You use less force to lift the load because the doorknob holds some of the load's weight.

Compound Pulleys

You can make your work even easier if you use a compound pulley. A compound pulley is two or more pulleys working together. You can make a compound pulley. You just need to add a fixed pulley to your movable pulley.

You made a fixed pulley before. It is the screwdriver with the spool on it. Hold the handle of the screwdriver against the doorknob. Have a friend hold both ends of the screwdriver in place.

Hold the screwdriver in place on the doorknob.

Put the string around the movable pulley. Then put the loose end of the string over the fixed pulley. It is very easy to raise and lower the load. The fixed pulley lets you pull downward with gravity. And the movable pulley makes the doorknob hold part of the weight of the load.

Raise and lower your load. You are still using about 3 units of force to lift the load. But the compound pulley makes your work easier because you are pulling down with gravity.

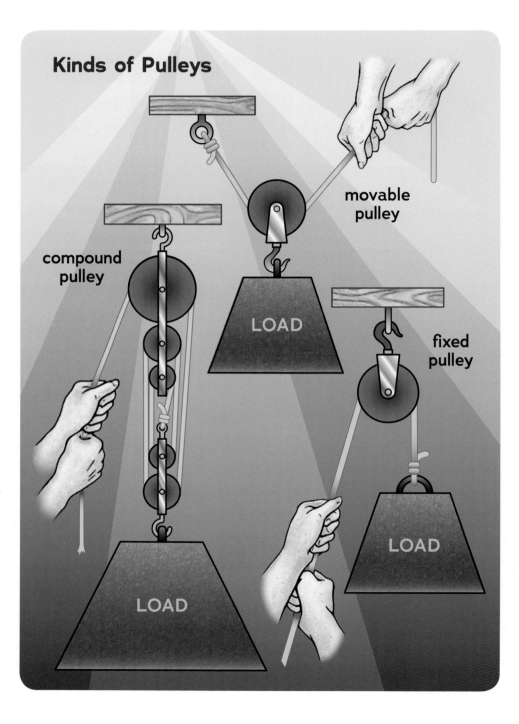

Kinds of Pulleys

movable pulley

compound pulley

LOAD

fixed pulley

LOAD

LOAD

Pulleys Make Work Easier

You have learned a lot about pulleys. Some pulleys change the direction of your force. Some pulleys let you use less force.

Using a pulley gives you an advantage. An advantage is a better chance of finishing your work. Using a pulley is almost like having a helper. That makes your work easier. And that is a real advantage.

This clothesline has a fixed pulley at the end. It makes it eaiser to move the clothes to take them down.

Glossary

complicated machine: a machine that has many moving parts

compound pulley: two or more pulleys working together

fixed pulley: a pulley that stays attached in one place

force: a push or a pull

friction: a force caused when two objects rub together

gravity: the force that pulls everything toward Earth

load: an object you want to move

movable pulley: a pulley that is attached to a load

pulley: a wheel that has a rope looped around it. The rope fits in a groove that runs around the edge of the wheel.

simple machine: a machine that has few moving parts

work: moving an object from one place to another

Learn More about Simple Machines

Books

Manolis, Kay. *Pulleys*. Minneapolis: Bellwether Media, 2010. Learn more about pulleys in this interesting introduction.

Volpe, Karen. *Get to Know Pulleys*. New York: Crabtree, 2009. This book discusses how pulleys work and how people use them.

Walker, Sally M., and Roseann Feldmann. *Put Wheels and Axles to the Test*. Minneapolis: Lerner Publications Company, 2012. Read all about wheels and axles, another simple machine.

Way, Steve, and Gerry Bailey. *Simple Machines*. Pleasantville, NY: Gareth Stevens, 2009. This title explores a variety of simple machines, from wheels and axles to ramps and levers.

Websites

Powerful Pulleys
http://library.thinkquest.org/CR0210120/Powerful%20P.html
Check out this website to read more about fixed pulleys, movable pulleys, and pulley systems.

Quia—Simple Machines
http://www.quia.com/quiz/101964.html
Visit this site to find a challenging interactive quiz that allows budding physicists to test their knowledge of simple machines.

Simple Machines
http://sln.fi.edu/qa97/spotlight3/spotlight3.html
This site features brief information about simple machines and helpful links you can click on to learn more.

Index

Photo Acknowledgments

Photographs copyright © Andy King. Additional images are used with the permission of: © Monkey Business Images/Dreamstime.com, p. 4; © Andrew Errington/Photographer's Choice/Getty Images, p. 6; © moodboard/SuperStock, p. 26; © Laura Westlund/Independent Picture Service, p. 36; © iStockphoto.com/lamiel, p. 37.

Front cover: © iStockphoto.com/Kerstin Klaassen.

Main body text set in Adrianna Regular 14/20.
Typeface provided by Chank.